T0065206

SPIRIT WATCHING

Learning to See
Ghosts, Earth Spirits and Others

PART I

FIRST, CONQUER FEAR

Catherine Espara

SPIRIT WATCHING
LEARNING TO SEE GHOSTS, EARTH SPIRITS AND OTHERS
PART I – FIRST, CONQUER FEAR

iUniverse books may be ordered through booksellers or by contacting:

iUniverse
1663 Liberty Drive
Bloomington, IN 47403
www.iuniverse.com
844-349-9409

Because of the dynamic nature of the Internet, any web addresses or links contained in
this book may have changed since publication and may no longer be valid. The views
expressed in this work are solely those of the author and do not necessarily reflect the
views of the publisher, and the publisher hereby disclaims any responsibility for them.

Any people depicted in stock imagery provided by Getty Images are models,
and such images are being used for illustrative purposes only.
Certain stock imagery © Getty Images.

ISBN: 978-1-6632-2819-2 (sc)
ISBN: 978-1-6632-2820-8 (e)

Library of Congress Control Number: 2021917627

Print information available on the last page.

iUniverse rev. date: 09/13/2021

TABLE OF CONTENTS

NOTE FROM THE AUTHOR

I wrote this for anyone who has seen something that was "just their imagination" – yet, it lingers in memory as if to insist on reconciliation. I wrote it for seers interested in another balanced and sane perspective and for readers ready to have their own experience.

Tales of spirit beings are part of human social history, existing in cultures of nearly all people over all time. There are stories of nature's spirits, ancestors, prophets, and gods roaming the Earth barely out of sight. No matter what interpretation is stated or learned, humans have always seen spirits on Earth.

I allowed the visions of other-dimensional beings whenever they appeared. I even encouraged the encounters. Resolving my fear, I questioned dogma, myth, and superstition, considering alternative perspectives on evil and darkness as they emerged. I sought to isolate imagination, both my own and that of others, to clear the way to witness a phenomenon at its source. I discovered that the exploration of these, mostly invisible, supernatural beings is both possible and safe.

Spirit Watching has no ritual, no study, and no doctrines. The practice stems from a personal exploration rooted in chance encounters and the circumstance of freedom of thought in a unique time and place. Over the years, I uncovered layers of fear affecting my willingness to see what was there to be seen.

I've had experiences of allies and guides, masters of magnificent benevolence, and sometimes a terrifyingly wrathful essence. Angels, extraterrestrials, apparitions, deva, and deities of the Earth are all accessible while spirit watching. Letting go of memory and imagination, I listen; seeking them, seeing them, getting to know them without deciding what, or who, they are.

That said, for the purpose of communication after the fact, I don't seem to be able to refrain from naming some entities based on attributes similar to those described in fiction, myth, and the belief systems of others. For example, in the context of my work, the word *ghost* is intended only as a literary tool, not as any particular definition as you might assume. Whatever you think when you see the word can be inserted, including "that which I do not see or believe exists."

I have trouble finding words to share these experiences. Many descriptions are laden with superstition, fiction, and dogma. Calling these entities *supernatural* seems to create a bridge between words used over millennia and words that most aptly describe the phenomena. These are beings composed of subtle energy, otherworldly, having an essence of individual personality. They are entities becoming visible or invisible according to spatial laws I don't understand.

At the very least, the beings I encounter appear to be centers of intelligence, each in its own right, alert to a point of view seemingly other than my own. I notice the characteristics and attitudes of these entities when I find them. They have form and position and sometimes a discernible attitude. Naturally, I want to know what is happening when I have these supernatural encounters.

And, so it began. I chose to temporarily put aside the idea that the persistent visions of my childhood were simply my imagination. Curious, I explored the visions, thinking they would at least lead to a deeper understanding of myself. As I navigated these mostly solitary personal explorations, fear was my persistent companion; even into adulthood, controlled or not, fear was always there.

As I unravel these experiences today, I find my observations may be quite different from yours. The personal quality inherent in the supernatural experience challenges me to temporarily release the beliefs I unwittingly cling to as I go. I've chosen to consciously clear my prejudice and get closer to whatever is there to be seen.

My purpose is to add to the store of knowledge rather than confuse it for the sake of entertainment. I would have enjoyed writing creative endings for these frightening accounts. I love exciting stories forged in my imagination or the creative foundries of others — this is not one of those.

All I can do is to strive for a clear and accurate account of what I have seen and what I thought about it at the time. As you may know, every brush with a spirit being does not necessarily make a profound story. So, I share the mundane and anticlimactic endings as they happened, without fiction or exaggerated levity.

In my approach to *Spirit Watching,* you will find open-minded freedom encouraging your personal experiences as I share mine. Together, we can discover more about what is there to be seen when memory and imagination are subdued, even if for a moment.

INTRODUCTION
First, Conquer Fear

*Each time I tamed a bit of fear, I
experienced greater freedom.*

Right at the onset of a possible encounter, fear catches my breath
and holds it. It keeps me at bay, causing me to hide, making
me want to turn and run away. If you haven't experienced this
kind of reaction to the supernatural, credit your lucky stars.
Many people feel apprehensive, excited and even terrified in
the presence of mysterious, barely perceptible, unknown forces.

This is a nonfiction account of my journey to overcome the
fear of supernatural beings. I'm still processing the significance
or folly of pursuing the visions at all. I think it is possible to
grow up fine, disregarding every glimpse, passing them off
as imagination. I just couldn't hide my terror and ignore my
curiosity.

As you might imagine, over the years, I've had plenty of
opportunity to reflect on my own fear reactions. As I indulged
my curiosity regarding otherworldly visions, I identified this list
of four main categories most likely to affect my actions:

1. **Intuitive warning of danger** – heightened alertness
   regarding the source and character of some imminent
   threat, resulting in courage or retreat.

2. **Subconscious memory of primal or recent trauma** – charged, involuntary reaction to an occurrence, resulting in an inability to evaluate the current situation accurately.
3. **Conditioned belief** – persistent reinforcement of a learned idea, resulting in the uncontested expectation of promised pain, suffering or reward.
4. **Imagination** – sublimely fearsome fiction, resulting in confusion about the actual danger inherent in a situation, sight or sound.

The first step in learning to see ghosts, earth spirits, and others is to identify and conquer some probable fears. In my exploration of the supernatural, I've had to look deeply into my reactive behaviors, discovering for myself the source of dread and alarm in each encounter.

Before I begin describing my personal experience of each of these types of fear, I want to take a moment to emphasize an awareness of personal responsibility. I can only know my own experience regarding spirit watching. I invite you to yours with this one small reminder.

Be Safe

Getting lost or hurt are real dangers to be avoided. I'm sure you can imagine how easy it might be to get lost in the darkness while following the subtle beckoning of a spirit being. If you decide to try some of the techniques described in this book, I hope you will initiate your safety measures before pushing yourself into action. A walk into the old memories of a nearby urban landscape or an unfamiliar wilderness has its own perils.

Naturally, I would not propose to have any uncommon advice to offer if you are confronted by a tangible, apparent danger—a predator, human or animal; a slippery cliff or crumbling rock; rotting stairs and floors. In such cases, you must use your wits to keep yourself safe by whatever means appropriate. When possible, evaluate these conditions before you go. In an unexpected predicament, breathe, gather your thoughts to identify the threat and act decisively to get free from the danger. Please, be safe in the physical world.

When confronted with the fear of the supernatural, be willing to control your reactions long enough to see what's there. Running in the dark in a state of terror and confusion can easily lead to serious injury. Sometimes those immediate reactions are stimulated by remembered fiction, or sometimes by deeply rooted ideas regarding evil, darkness, horror, and damnation. From my experience, I can confidently suggest that, with regard to seeing disembodied spirits of people, nature and others— breathe. Don't run!

CHAPTER 1
Too Scared to Move

I suppose we all react to a surge of terror in different ways. For me, I just can't move. I'm paralyzed. I find myself holding my breath as if to be so quiet and motionless that I might become invisible myself. I don't scream. I don't run.

As a child, I wondered if I dared to look at what was causing my terror. I was afraid on so many levels as I unwittingly began this journey of discovery. I remember lying in bed, quivering under the covers—barely able to breathe and praying for protection from this evil.

Ghost in the Farmhouse

In 1961, my family moved to an old farmhouse in Kansas. The land around our property was mostly flat, with creeks running through shallow gorges etched into the sloping banks on an otherwise featureless landscape. Rows of corn, milo and alfalfa grew along both sides of the straight road extended for a mile in all four directions. Osage hedgerows outlined fields and farms with dark green borders.

The weathered two-story farmhouse fronted sagging outbuildings and a large barn making up the main homesite. Near the driveway, a shrub-lined walkway led to an iron hand pump centered on a concrete slab.

Just beyond was a house built sometime in the 19th century by men who also built a barn with beams fitted with wooden pegs and angled inserts. They forged and hammered square nails to use in the horse stalls and sliding doors.

My awakening to the phenomena of the ghost haunting the farmhouse was progressive over the years we lived there. It's hard to remember the first experience exactly. I do remember my uncontrollable quivering as I lay awake, cowering in a tight fetal position under the covers in my bedroom at the end of the upstairs hallway. It was always very late at night while everyone in the family was asleep.

These frightful experiences always began in the same way. I climbed to the midpoint of the stairway and paused to lean over the banister to utter my goodnights to the family. Carrying my cat, I ascended the final steps in the bedtime routine.

On a few nights of the year, my cat would suddenly begin a desperate struggle to free himself from my arms just as we crested the floor of the second level of the house. That cat would stop nothing short of clawing and growling as he slipped from my grasp and raced to a hiding place in some unknown corner of the kitchen pantry. I was bewildered by my pet's behavior and felt hurt rather than alarmed.

Feeling nothing unusual otherwise, I snuggled into my bed, lights out, peacefully drifting into sleep. Then, on some nights, something caused me to awaken when there was nothing there at all. Over time, I noticed that the cat's odd behavior seemed to precede these eerie awakenings during the night.

Having been suddenly awakened by what seemed to be nothing at all, I naturally opened my eyes to see if anything was there. The feeling in the room was different on these nights. I remember my heart pounding, goosebumps prickling on my arms, my mind racing with justifications and explanations as I tried to extinguish the rush of sensation. Breathless, I felt uncommon alertness that could only accompany some notion of fright or impending doom. I was frightened, and I didn't know why.

Motionless, I strained my ears to listen for a clue to suddenly having been awakened. The feelings were so powerful that I covered my head and shook uncontrollably under the blankets. Holding in my breath and squeezing my eyes shut, I went right to the source every time. "Oh God, protect me from evil, protect me from evil," I prayed with all my conviction.

And . . . eventually, I would fall back to sleep.

As this continued over the years, I became impatient at the idea that I was suffering such unreasonable fear of nothing at all. I vowed to clear my mind of whatever I was so frightened of. During this period, I imagined I was suffering from a childhood dilemma not much different from the illogical fear the boogeyman or monster in the closet. I was nine at the time; too old, I thought, to have such terrifying experiences of imagined terror.

I knew nothing about psychology. Scattered about my bedroom were stuffed animals sitting on tiny chairs, flowers, goldfish, and all the things that made me happy. I was a normal young girl living with my family in an aging Midwestern farmhouse.

3

Even as a child, I intuitively understood that these experiences of terror could be signs of a mental problem. I made a commitment to myself to handle it before anyone else knew about it. This choice added to a sense of aloneness and vulnerability I felt as a young girl. I began hiding what I thought and felt.

After several of these nocturnal episodes of quaking terror—and with all the courage I could muster—I finally began to quiver with my head above the covers and my eyes open. I dared to breathe, loosening the grip of terror on my stiffened body. I barely made a sound as my eyes searched all the corners of the room in a concentrated gaze. I wanted to see into the darkness of the night and discover the source of this feeling of terror. I was convinced there was something there.

I tried softening my focus to see into the darkness. This soft focus was something I had practiced, alone, in my bedroom—trying to sleep on any night of the year. I suppose I was curious about superpowers. I remember using the wooden frame around a single pane of window glass as a focal point and contrasting the sight of the leaves and branches on the tree beyond. If I looked just so, I could see one leaf but not another. If I looked with an opposite dominant focus, I could see the other leaf but not the now invisible ones I saw before. As I balanced the focus from both perspectives, I thought I might be learning to see through things.

Now I tried using this dubious skill, not focusing on anything, balancing left/right peripheral vision, as I slowly gazed around my bedroom, scanning from corner to corner. Most of the time, I saw nothing, and eventually, the alertness dissipated, leaving sleepy questions rolling slowly through my mind as I settled again under the covers.

The first sighting I can remember was a wisp of light rising from the baseboard along a wall opposite the foot of the bed. As I watched, it slowly grew several feet in height and wavered there. The edges were inconsistent and not particularly discernible. Immediately, I had the idea that this could be a ghost. With renewed terror, I covered my head and shook until I finally fell back to sleep.

The next specific memory I have of the ghost in the farmhouse started in a similar way. While I gazed around the room, a wisp of light appeared and began to take shape. This time, instead of hiding, I looked for an explanation. Perhaps a car was passing along the road in the distance, shining diffused headlights through the windows and onto the wall. I now had enough control over my fear to look away from the form wavering on the wall and search the outdoors for a light source. I saw nothing.

The house was half a mile from the nearest neighbor. Flat Kansas terrain made it easy to see headlights in any direction, the moonlight shining through the trees, or clouds passing in the sky. No light, reflection, or known source of illumination could be found in my upstairs room that night, even as I purposefully looked for it.

Still, the wisp of light wavered on the wall, slowly moving in different directions, periodically phasing in and out of sight. After a few of these sightings, I realized my worst fear had become concretely and obviously true - a ghost was haunting my bedroom.

Unfortunately, I didn't take it well. Validating the presence of the supernatural created overwhelming terror, demanding immediate relief. I spontaneously used a strong, silent intention, commanding the spirit to leave. "Get out of here," I screamed frantically from within.

The form disappeared, and along with the disappearance went my terror and dread. The uncomfortable body sensations dissipated. I was no longer quivering and breathing shallow breaths. There in my bedroom, late in the night, the panic was gone.

I remember feeling some sadness at having ended the encounter. I realized that I had been in no mortal danger after all and that I had the power to stop an experience if necessary. I was curious about what I had seen and wondered if it had been a ghost or possibly an angel. I used that same strong, commanding intention to communicate that I wanted to see it again. The ghost didn't come back that night, nor did it return for more than a year. I thought I would never see it again.

Then, one night, I awakened to a touch on my cheek. When my eyes popped open, I glimpsed a white flash in my periphery. Abruptly, I sat up to see what it was, already feeling the apprehension and dread I had become so familiar with. I held my breath, barely allowing the air to escape, and listened for the slightest sound. There was only silence—although something was different at this moment. As familiar as the chilling encounters had become, this time, the feeling was of imminent closeness.

The touch had not been a familiar feeling. I remember it as barely there, not the creeping touch of a spider or the gentle touch of my mother. It was different, more electric, not so powerful as a static zap. My skin was prickling with goosebumps, particularly my face. I rubbed my cheek to get rid of the tingling feeling while the flush of fear continued to spread over me. I tried to remember everything about the moment I had awakened. This feeling was not like a lingering dream. Awake and watchful, I waited.

My rational mind began its business of explaining the event in terms I could accommodate. It must have been the curtains next to my bed responding to a sudden breeze coming through the windowsill. In the winter, the old farmhouse windows were covered with plastic, nailed to the trim from the outside with neat rows of stripping. This kept the cold out and helped the unheated bedrooms on the second floor maintain enough warmth from downstairs to be bearable through the night. The source of the flash I witnessed when I first opened my eyes was not likely a curtain blowing in the wind.

Could it have been someone in my family creeping in to check on me? The creaky boards of that old house told of even the slightest shift of weight when my brothers and I played hide and seek. The silence I heard as I listened could only be the silence of an empty hallway. No sound had accompanied the swiftness of the flash of white when I first awoke. It had been a touch and a glimpse without sound or explanation.

I laid back and slowly slid deep beneath the covers, alert and watching. For several tense minutes, I lay there expecting to see the ghost again. I could only *hear the pounding of my heart and the quiet shallow gasps of my breath as I listened intently for more clues.*

I remember drifting off to sleep with the idea that what I had seen had been the curtains after all. I felt safe with this explanation—until I woke the following day and remembered what had happened. I immediately checked the curtains, looking for facts.

As far as I could tell, there was no noticeable leak in the window plastic. I gently swung the curtain out to see if the dust would easily fall from the cotton ruffle. It did, proving the unlikeliness that the curtains had been recently disturbed. I felt a bit queasy as I remembered the events in the night and realized I could find no reasonable explanation for what I had experienced. It seemed a ghost had touched me, and it had a lasting, profound effect on me.

These experiences tormented me as a child. Schizophrenia was a term I had heard thrown around as an insult on the playground. I had no idea what it meant other than it seemed to be a synonym for crazy. Naturally, I didn't want anyone to know I might be afflicted, so I didn't tell the story. I was young and not so brave and self-assured as I would have liked to have been. Looking back, I realize that hiding my experience of the supernatural was usually my first instinct. There was no reason to discuss it.

One final notation on the haunting is technically just hearsay. I came home from school one day and was told that my mother and brother had heard a faint whistling of an Irish tune from upstairs. Surprisingly, my mother felt there was no threat in the possible presence of a ghost in the house. Her acceptance gave my own experience some degree of legitimacy. If mom wasn't frightened, maybe I didn't need to be either. If mom accepted the possibility of a ghost, maybe I wasn't crazy after all.

In retrospect, I count my mother's ability to accept the unexplained as one of the fortunate circumstances of my life. This quietly devoted woman encountered a specter in her historic home years later. From time to time, someone of an ethereal nature sat on her bed, seemingly to rest while recalling a memory. She remained nonchalant regarding these experiences and exhibited an acceptance I admired.

CHAPTER 2
Discoveries of a Young Girl

Of course, there are more ghost stories. Such stories are easily found in hundreds of thousands of accounts throughout the written traditions of virtually all cultures. Whether enhanced by the diversity of these stories or cheapened by it, the varying accounts represent a human fascination for supernatural beings, ancestors, and monsters.

I didn't know what to think. I was intrigued by the experience and took every opportunity to practice breathing through that terrible inability to move or think during a possible encounter. Eventually, paralysis was less of an issue. I made progress, learning from experience, noticing fear was always there to contend with.

Boogeyman under the Bed

I had the boogeyman under the bed syndrome in that very bedroom of that same farmhouse. I suffered my own monster behind exposed hanging clothes at the far end of the room. I think most of us know how it goes. It starts with a glimpse of a shadow or movement. Then an anxiousness develops, escalating to a nearly unbearable level. It can be overwhelming.

I recall anticipating what gruesome menace I would see when it came for me. I imagined the look of supernatural forces and spirit presence. I had images, horrible images, derived from remembered art, fiction, and superstition. I'm not surprised I was so frightened of what I thought was lurking just out of sight. I didn't want to see it. I hoped it would not come out in the open—not ever.

When I was engaged with the boogeyman fright, my mind was fully activated, informing the rest of me to anticipate something dreadful. I realized the idea of the appearance of the object of my horror seemed to be coming from my creative memory, something thought rather than perceived at the moment.

At first, I had been startled. Then the thoughts took over, generating the panicky fear characteristic of the whole boogeyman affliction. Alone, in my bedroom in the dark, I handled my fear in all the ways I knew would help, breathing and praying for protection.

Alternately, the feelings I had as a young girl becoming aware of the specter wavering on the wall at the foot of my bed were different. While I had been too frightened to look initially, this soon changed to a cautious curiosity, stimulated by prickly skin, shallow breath, and a heightened sense of alertness.

Unlike the boogeyman terror, there was no anticipated horror just out of sight. I didn't have an image of what I might see, and I didn't have the notion it was hiding. Instead, the ghost experiences were alarming body sensations, catching me off-guard, a physical reaction to something my mind hadn't figured out yet. My *terror had an inquisitive characteristic. "What is this? What's happening?"*

Without the simultaneous occurrences of the boogeyman incidents and the sightings of the ghost, I might not have had my first inspiration concerning imagination and perception. I could feel the difference, and it stirred my curiosity even more. There was an adventure and a mystery to unravel.

The Ouija Scare

There were some early indications I may have been given subtle permission to allow unusual perceptions. For Christmas in 1958, I received an Ouija board, a large cardboard puppet theater, and a doll that smelled like a new shower curtain. I don't particularly remember playing with the Ouija board much at that time. It was a child's game full of imagination and mysterious magic — much like the eight ball floating answers to a window as questions are asked.

Three years later, after we moved to that old farmhouse, mom and I occasionally played with the Ouija board. We mostly asked yes/no or number questions, even though I now had the skills to read. "How many eggs will I collect tomorrow?" The answer often proved to be spot on, creating just enough mystery to be exciting. Against this background of occasionally confirmed accuracy, the Ouija board was still very much a toy, a source of entertainment.

One night, the outcomes went far beyond the simple directional responses we asked for. Our arms yanked this way and that as we struggled to keep our fingertips relaxed over the heart-shaped disk floating over the figures on the board. Not being particularly alarmed and hardly believing mom thought I would fall for this little trick, I helped solve the puzzles as letters came through the little window. Sentences were spelled out. I thought it was my mom entertaining me.

Suddenly, she gasped and jumped up. I had no idea why. When I asked, she just said, "Never mind. It's nothing." That night, mom took the Ouija board outside and threw it into the flames of the incinerator barrel. Her behavior was bewildering to me. It upset me, and I tried to figure out what had caused her to destroy my game.

Soon, my dad made it clear that it was nothing. "That kinda talk is horse shit," I heard him say to mom. "Don't be saying that crap around here." I didn't talk with my parents about my experiences of the ghost in the upstairs bedroom.

I didn't know what to think in those early years, so I thought about angels and dead people. Nothing in my naïve spiritual repertoire was adequate to explain what I was experiencing. I began to accept that I was an adolescent girl who was seeing ghosts. In my rural American world, information was sparse and unreliable. When it came to the supernatural, I figured I was pretty much on my own.

A Séance Indeed

At some point, it occurred to me that I might gain a unique status among the other children due to the discovery of my ability to see ghosts. I decided to share with some of my friends, conveying a hint of bragging along with the creation of some innocently contrived connecting stories. At a slumber party, I agreed to participate in a séance. We were inexperienced, giddy little girls looking for something exciting to add to our evening.

We sat in a circle and held hands while we attempted to "contact" the spirit world. There was no intention around who we might bring forth and no idea what our purpose would be if we were successful. We were going through the motions much as we would have if we had donned high heels and mom's most extravagant hat. It was all for fun.

Our biggest challenge was to stop giggling. I was the leader by default. Although I don't remember it, I can imagine that I behaved as if I knew more than I actually did. We needed to be quiet, close our eyes, and concentrate. Finally, we were all engaged in meditative behavior, although I have no idea what anyone, including myself, was concentrating on.

Soon, I opened my eyes just a bit and began to scan the room with a soft focus. I noticed some wavering energy at the end of the large rectangular table. It had a familiar quality, a barely visible image on a radiating canvas of indiscernible waves. I told the girls that I saw a man standing in the room with a beard and white hair. "He's a good spirit, with a narrow face," I proclaimed as if I knew beyond a doubt what was there.

I made it up. I didn't see features in this vision with any more clarity than the familiar wisp on my bedroom wall. For some reason, the presence of my audience must have spurred a disposition in me to embellish the encounter. I'd seen something for sure, and I wanted to speak out and be heard. I imagined what I had seen and told the story with an air of certainty. I couldn't have predicted the result of my carelessness.

One of the girls screamed, threw a pillow at me, and hid her face in her hands. There were terrified expressions jumbled with cries of surprise and disbelief. Hysteria accompanied the shrieks of little girls as if a contagious wave of terror and excitement poured over the room.

Of course, the vision disappeared, and the moment was brought to a sudden halt. My friend was crying and talking about her grandfather, who had recently passed away. There was something about the look in my eyes, a glassy stare, which had frightened some of the girls. They looked at me as if I had done something terribly dangerous, as if I was an embodiment of some vague, forbidden notion.

A picture brought down from upstairs confirmed that my pretend description of the visiting spirit was spot on, a weird coincidence that confused me. Perhaps I really did see that much and was suffering denial—believing I had only imagined the outlines and personality. Perhaps the concentration of the granddaughter during the little ceremony implanted images telepathically. I don't have any answers. We *stopped the séance and moved on to something more appropriate—a round of Twister.*

Later the same year, at another slumber party with some of the same girls, we tried it again. This time I imagined I saw an image of a little girl who looked very much like our hostess with different hair color. Again, there were screams and cries, little girls covering their eyes and hiding their faces in the pillows. This time the story was of a girl's sister, a fair-haired version of herself, who had drowned in the pool not many years before. I was shown a picture of the two girls taken before the accident, and I, too, was a bit shaken.

I couldn't understand the confirmation of made-up details. This confusion prompted a private vow not to fabricate details again. Using imagination muffled the facts, I could understand this. The problem was the unexpected confirmations, leaving me even more confused about the nature of the supernatural. I felt I was getting nowhere with my efforts to gain a greater understanding.

Now I had a reputation among the young people at school. The questionable status I had achieved led me to keep my fascination with supernatural visions a secret once more. Simply allowing the visions to exist felt as if I was running some kind of risk. To be sure, there was a strong sense of self-preservation in my secrecy. I still had to survive high school.

Once my family moved from that farmhouse, the ghostly visits ended abruptly. They became vivid memories, while my sensitivity lingered as if it had become a part of me. The sensation was mostly the prickly feeling of the hairs on my arms and the back of my neck. Those creepy feelings are easily brushed off and forgotten.

Sometimes it was a sudden unexplained chill, a flash in my periphery, or a wisp in the darkness where it ought not to be. Almost always accompanied by a sense of dread, these instances often left me hoping and wishing it was just my imagination.

"By replacing fear of the unknown with curiosity we open ourselves up to an infinite stream of possibility."

- Alan Watts

CHAPTER 3
Noticing Fear of the Unknown

I think we may all have some fear of the dark. Our evolution among nocturnal predators would surely have spawned a deeply rooted fear of the night, of the unknown. I think it's under my skin, deep in my consciousness. If I don't know what it is, where it is, if it is, then it unnerves me. I may be startled into acute alertness at a glimpse of movement I barely see or an unexpected sound I didn't hear before. Even the squeak of a door hinge loosened by a breeze can invoke this feeling of sudden terror when I'm alone in the dark.

I practice walking to learn more about my fear of the dark. On these occasions, I seek a feeling of safety in the dark rather than the challenge of supernatural visions. Sometimes it's difficult to establish a dependable safety zone where I can sense the darkness in peace. When I notice this, I usually stay at home. Choosing to practice with a companion amenable to exploring natural reactions to darkness will still mute certain sensations stimulated by the vulnerability of being alone.

I examine my sensations as I walk in the night. The feelings are those of alertness to the presence of animals and apprehension of something unknown. By becoming familiar with these sensations, I can isolate them during a spirit watching session. Separating fear of the dark from the experience of a spirit entity nearby will help me understand the signals generated by my body and help me calm myself.

The story of the sinkhole is not about fear of darkness. Unbridled fear of the unknown overwhelmed reasonable exploration and completely squelched an opportunity to uncover the facts surrounding a local myth. I ran away, seeing nothing, learning nothing.

Legend of the Sinkhole

In 1971, during my early college days, I decided to tell a particularly close friend about my experiences with supernatural explorations. He was intrigued and remembered a mysterious story he thought I might be interested in investigating. Tom took me to a place in the southern Missouri hills where folks talked about a monster in the woods, trapped in a sinkhole. We drove for some time from the little college town of Rolla to get to the cabin of an old-timer who knew the rumored location of this legendary monster.

When we arrived, we were greeted by a leathery, self-styled woodsman, his demeanor unexpectedly gracious and welcoming. As we entered his small home, my attention was immediately drawn to the shelves of unusual natural objects, animal skeletons, and scruffy displays lining every wall of the otherwise cozy room. Noticing my intrigue, Tom's friend shared some stories, including one of the illusive jackalope. "Few have ever seen one," he said.

The old man walked to a wall of shelves on the other side of the room. "Here's a skull of one," he remarked as he pointed to a tiny antlered head displayed among small mammal skeletons and pieces of unusually shaped wood.

"Jackalopes really do exist, you know. They look like a rabbit with tiny antlers," the old-timer continued with a convincingly serious tone.

I didn't want to be the fool, yet I didn't want to offend our host before he gave us the sinkhole location. I was in an uncomfortable position and could only smile as if I understood the joke. He didn't let up.

"Are you going to refute the evidence just to protect your belief that they don't exist?" he asked, gesturing at the skull with an abrupt invitation. I carefully eyed the artifact. The tiny skull had antlers anchored in a perfect organic form, much like the antlers of a deer, although impossibly small. I already knew there was no such creature, so it didn't matter how perfect the specimen seemed. There could obviously be no valid evidence of the mythical jackalope.

In light of this complex hoax, I knew the chances that there was really a monster in a sinkhole were slim at best. Once we had heard the tale of the monster, complete with our host's eyewitness account, we were ready to explore the site ourselves. It was nearly dusk when we found ourselves alone in the woods that night.

In the Missouri hills, a sinkhole often refers to an area of ground dropped into the labyrinth of collapsing caves below the surface. A sinkhole is generally characterized by steep cliffs surrounding a sunken chunk of land. Usually, they are roughly defined and partially filled with water.

After quietly stalking the location through tall spindly trees and thick crinkling leaf cover, we came upon a huge, pot-shaped hole, perhaps 200 feet wide and at least 30 feet deep. From what I could see that night, trees and bushes grew on the bottom of the sunken platform on the forest floor. We explored a bit and agreed the edges were steep and would be hazardous in the dark. We settled on a comfortable spot on the perimeter to sit and listen.

We waited, sitting quietly for what seemed like a very long time as dusk turned into night and the sounds of the natural woods transformed little noises into larger ones while obvious sounds turned quiet. Listening to the slow rhythm of the changes relaxed the anxiety of being in the woods at night. Then suddenly, there was a cracking sound from within the sinkhole. It was immediately terrifying.

From the sounds, I imagined the "monster" was large, perhaps the size of a bear, or a buck or a cow. It crashed around at an aggressive pace, heavily disrupting the opposite side of the sunken geologic area. I tried all the animal images I could think of, listening and fitting the sounds into a form of what seemed possible.

I remember becoming frightened, unable to discern what was down there, trapped by the steep sides of the sinkhole. At one point, the sounds stopped, and it became very quiet as we whispered to each other in exciting confirmation of what we had heard. We sat *still, as if frozen to the spot, barely breathing, hearts pounding.*

After a while, we heard a thudding sound approaching from across the sunken floor ending in a rustling of branches right below the cliff where we sat. The sound of the thudding confused me. This was no four-legged hoofed animal plodding through the bushes. There weren't likely to be bears in these parts, and it was even less likely one would come lumbering across the forested floor on two legs.

We jumped up, realizing we may have been found out. I quickly succumbed to the growing anxiety, desperately trying to fill in an explanation. I didn't want whatever was down there to know we were there. Perhaps it wasn't trapped at all.

"We have to go now," I pleaded with terrified urgency. We did go—as fast as we could get back to the car.

This ended the adventure with just enough information about the monster in the sinkhole to keep the myth alive. I tried to explain the pieces of the experience that didn't fit. Maybe in that cavernous basin, the sounds reverberated in unexpected ways, prompting illusions and echoed thumps. Perhaps I was the unsuspecting victim of another hoax. The legend of MoMo sprang from a movie at just about the same time in a nearby Missouri county.

In the end, I denied myself the satisfaction of knowing more about the monster by allowing fear of the unknown to overtake me. I wondered if this deeply rooted fear of the unknown could be a boundary I would not be able to overcome.

The next year my life abruptly changed. I married and moved to Oregon, where I studied massage and bodywork. I heard about energy meridians flowing through the body and breath as a source of life-force.

I learned muscles and connective tissue store emotional and mental trauma. Having been shocked or traumatized, subtle aspects of the tissues can become resistant, guiding energy around the site of the stored blockage. Movement, posture, health, and wellbeing can all be affected. Realizing the link between movement and past trauma led me to consider a relationship between the gripping breathlessness of fear and past shocking or terrifying events.

About this same time, I came across one of the many New Age groups popping up in the American counter-culture. Amid other recommendations, Leonard Orr, the founder of Theta Seminars, advocated the release of stored primal trauma, believing it blocked the free flow of life force, known as Chi, or breath. Apparently, Leonard had discovered a technique to connect to a part of the psyche holding primal memories.

For years, I worked to understand the power of trauma within myself. I suspected my deepest fears originated in the primal pages of subliminal memory, leading back to my greatest experience of the unknown—the moment of being born.

This is the only story in this volume that is not about the supernatural. This is an account of a healing practice that seems to have affected my willingness to look deeply into the shadows. There was a new sense of safety in the resolution of original nonverbal decisions about life

It felt wrong not to include this information when considering the fear of the unknown.

Clearing Primal Trauma, Theta Style

It was called Rebirthing. I have always hated using that name for this relatively simple process since this practice is unburdened by the religious undertones I associate with the "reborn." The process was created by Leonard Orr and polished by many wonderful Rebirthers over years of practice. I first met Leonard in Eugene, Oregon, in 1974. I was fascinated by the Five Biggies he formulated to clear the way for Western seekers to master being alive.

Leonard talked about parental disapproval, birth trauma, specific negatives, unconscious death urge, and past lifetime trauma. I listened to his lectures and basically understood his unconventional logic.

"I am alive. Therefore, my urge to be alive is greater than my desire to die. As long as I go on increasing my life urge and decreasing my death urge, I will go on living in health and vitality."

Practicing affirmations to counteract some of the entrenched subconscious imprinting was central, although the key to the transformation seemed to be the Rebirthing.

In those early days, a session started with a discussion of the birth process. We read from an article in Redbook about a French obstetrician (Dr. Frederick Leboyer, author of <u>Birth Without Violence</u>). He thought of the newborn as a superconscious being, practically unlimited in the impressions of preverbal sensation gleaned in the moments preceding the first breath and continuing through the excruciating routines of being born.

A newborn might be smacked, dangling upside down by the heels, isolated, and subjected to bright lights and medical procedures without consideration for pain and distress. The interview with Dr. Leboyer suggested the newborn feels everything without censor or contextual framework.

The sessions were simple enough. Initially, I sat quietly and focused on my breath. This was the first instruction after the reading from the folded, water-rippled magazine. The requested practice was to inhale until my lungs were full and the natural urge of my entire torso was to exhale, which I allowed to happen without resistance.

It's all about allowing my body to breathe fully by not interfering—in a circle breath, completely full at the top of the circle, letting the natural exhale take over until a great sigh empties my lungs to the bottom of the imaginary circle. Sweeping around the bottom curve and back to the top, a natural inhale drops my diaphragm and expands my chest, allowing the rush of air back into my lungs.

The prescribed conditions are met when the inhale is again fully flowing over the top of the circle and softly swooping the bottom without a hitch in the flow. Completely rhythmic and smooth, my breath overtakes my sense of control. I let my body breathe itself. I am ready for the second part of the process.

Now I am submerged naked into a large tub of warm water, just a degree or two above womb temperature, 102 or 103, face down with a snorkel. My attending Rebirther is more like a watcher, holding the snorkel to ensure that I am always breathing, that the snorkel is above water and that I am safe from interference. The presence of this overseer represents trust and safety as I descend into the calm darkness of the wooden hot tub.

Settling into a face-down position in the warm water, I can relax my arms, legs, shoulders, and neck. My well-trained Rebirther is breathing, too, staying neutral to my process. A touch or a soft squeeze of tightened muscles prompts attention to my stiffness and encourages letting go.

My attention is on an uninterrupted circle breath as I breathe through the snorkel with growing expertise, letting my head dangle from the tip of my spine, relaxing my breathing into a smooth rhythm. There is silence and patience, and I am safe to just breathe. Here, in the floatation and relaxation of the warm water, my spine naturally curves in a gentle arch from the tailbone to the skull. My head hangs loosely, as do my limbs to the tips of my fingers and toes.

My awareness drifts into wordless memories, buried so deeply they could be a dream. I allow these trails of thought wrapped in vivid feelings without definition, understanding or meaning, always aware of the rhythmic circular breath—letting every thought flow past as it does.

There is a time of fear and urgency, crisis and pain. All of these memories roll past my mental window, coming in and out of view as frames of film streaming past a focal point, illuminating the images as they pass, apparently without cohesion or continuity.

Suddenly, I feel panic and am sure I must surface immediately. I simply cannot be here a moment more, or I think I will surely die. The Rebirther, noticing the change in my breathing, breathes with me, gently encouraging a balanced circle breath, exhaling in a great sigh and slowly inhaling. Unsettling formless memories begin to melt away. I sigh and pick up the comfortable rhythm of conscious exhales, returning to a full circle of breath—and again.

At some point, I can no longer tolerate the conditions. I must be free. I feel confined, earnestly prepared for change. Anxiety grows beyond endurance, exploding through my senses, overwhelming all other thoughts. At this point, the Rebirther helps me roll slowly over, with my face resting above water, my neck fully supported in the cradle of a firm, gentle palm, still floating in the warm buoyancy of the tub.

The snorkel disappears, and the panic begins to melt. Here, with encouragement from the one who holds me, I open my lungs to breathe more fully, experiencing the expansiveness of the room's atmosphere on my face.

My eyes burn from the light contrasting with the darkness of my underwater environment. I am shaking with the chill and the vast emptiness around me, void of the warm, moist closeness of the tub of warm water. This place is terrifyingly severed from all that was before. I am completely vulnerable, painfully overwhelmed by strange and unexpected sensations.

This time, the watcher helps me to a pleasant experience. I am safe; it is dark and quiet, and there are no sudden movements. Slowly, I begin to trust as I awaken to the awareness of this place. Breath is instinctual and easy. This time I am able to notice the questions coming naturally. "What is this? Where am I?"

From this vantage point, I begin to realize I have, indeed, made some fundamental mistakes in my preverbal decisions about life. I answered those questions with formulas similar to "Wherever it is, it is a place of boundless pain and isolation. In this place, I am afraid. I don't want to be here long." That was the gist of how I met life on Earth in the early fifties.

In this instant of profound awareness, still the same person — still me, the same one born — I challenge those decisions and begin to change them. I am in a world of support and love. I can feel it, and it is as significant and powerful to me now as any I have experienced before.

In this moment of diverse sensation, I am safe. I accept being vulnerable and lost without a conceptual understanding of any of this. Within minutes of the acceptance, the session is over. There is resting and attendance. I am calm and without fear or pain for now. Awareness settles in unevenly and eventually begins to dissipate as my feet find the floor.

It was beginning to be clear that deep memories might trigger the fear of the unknown within my subconscious. I wondered if I could become free of some of my fears by going back and reprogramming automated preverbal decisions at the foundation of my strategy for survival. It seemed logical. I made the effort.

After many sessions, I noticed the increasing trust of the world and my circumstances. The unknown was no longer automatically deemed inexplicably terrifying and dangerous. I don't know if I would have had the courage to look into the shadows seeking visions of the supernatural had it not been for this fundamental change in understanding. This awareness created a baseline of safety I hadn't realized was missing.

CHAPTER 4
Evil Spirit or Not So Much

Upon conquering some of those basic fear reactions to the unknown, I discovered yet another source of dread. Religious fear of damnation coupled with popularized images of horrible demons from hell lingered against my will. Art, the church, family, and legend all reinforced my reluctance to see what was there to be seen. I found a deeply rooted fear that I would be possessed or my free will would be taken from me without my knowledge or consent. The idea of evil spirits seemed to be stuck to my psyche with an ageless adhesive, refusing to give way to reason.

By the mid-seventies, my repertoire of personal supernatural experiences was still pretty much limited to seeing apparitions of one description or another. Meanwhile, I welcomed America's New Age movement embracing Eastern religion and native cultures worldwide to expand spiritual awareness. At the time, my inner skeptic assumed Earth-based religions and tribal myths were likely superstitions or religious dramatizations. I was interested, participating, and questioning, although not necessarily ready to jump on board.

Demon in the Garden

I am enchanted by the night, by the moonlight, the shadows, and the utter relaxation I feel when I witness the unfolding of the evening. I love to listen for the changes as dusk is left behind and darkness takes over. From within my own home, the chill of the night and a subliminal primal alertness associated with being in the darkness give way to a calm feeling of personal safety.

On that particular autumn night, I was standing in a darkened room of my home just outside Eugene, Oregon, gazing out a picture window over the poorly attended landscape of a large terraced garden. I enjoyed the view and meditated in silence and comfort. It seemed natural to scan the forms and shadows, looking for patterns to delight my sense of wonder and beauty.

Before long, a particularly darkened patch of the garden caught my attention. Wrapped in the feeling of safety created by the comfort of being indoors, I decided to take the opportunity to look deeply into its shadowy center. The notion sent a tingling sensation crawling over my scalp, a creepy anticipation I usually associate with a slightly dangerous act. Knowing I was in no real danger, I pushed past the physical symptoms of the moment, remembering to breathe.

As I gazed, I noticed a curious intensity in the shadow of a clump of bushes and withering stalks. I noticed dying branches with long, dry leaves dangling randomly from the bush, giving it a particularly shadowy and darkened appearance compared to the relatively visible moonlit shapes of the other vegetation. My usual rational attempt to discredit the perception of mysterious vibes was fully engaged. "There's nothing unusual happening here right now," I repeated to myself.

Then it occurred to me. I could try to see instead of trying not to see. I let my focus relax, gazing at the shadow as if looking through the darkness to its origin. Unlike squinting and staring at a sight to see it more clearly, this gaze was soft and less piercing, using extended periphery awareness to balance the position of sight to a single point resting at the center above my brow ridge.

(To practice extended periphery awareness, start by sitting comfortably, looking ahead, chin at a comfortable horizontal. Without moving, except perhaps the eyes themselves, see the entire left periphery. Then see the full right periphery with the same stillness, maintaining an unchanged expression and position. Now see the right and the left periphery at the same time while establishing awareness of a subtle illumination appearing in the space between.)

Almost immediately, I could make out bands of color arching over the darkest center of the shadow under the bush. The core seemed dense and compacted, especially when compared with the wavering, ethereal qualities I had witnessed with spectral forms I'd seen before. Even though all the physical sensations of a supernatural encounter were present, I was reluctant to think I was seeing a ghost in this random outdoor space. I was curious to see more and began countering my activated skepticism by clearing my thoughts and concentrating on the notion of allowing perception.

As I continued to gaze intently at the colorful bands emanating from the shadow of the bush, I began to see a hideous face taking form in the blackness beneath the colors. The face had a hooked beak as if a bird of prey, fangs, furry cheeks, horns, or perhaps erect, narrow ears.

Of course, I thought this was a hallucination and consciously began to consider what mental influences might be surfacing to create this image. At that very moment, during the heart-pounding vision of this terrifying being, I was overwhelmed by religious notions and images from myth and fiction. The idea of a demon circled my mind relentlessly. I stood there, terrified, unable to turn away.

Barely breathing, clinging to a skeptical disbelief, I allowed myself a moment to observe this frightening vision. I noticed an unusual clarity as I summoned the courage to look. The illumination radiating from the bands of color themselves distinguished the features of the hideous face I perceived. I peered as deeply as I dared.

Then the being moved, slowly animating the singularity of its dark form as it stretched from a squatting position under the bush. This unexpected and unwanted movement seemed to demonstrate independence from my thought and was so utterly shocking at that moment that I nearly fainted. The blood drained from my extremities, and a rush of fresh demon concepts filled my head despite all my efforts to suppress them. Entirely horrified, I felt I had to protect myself from this menacing being that I had stumbled upon during my naïve exploration of the spirit world.

"Get back," I screamed from within, making no sound except the gasp of my breath. I sent my demanding message quickly and firmly.

Since this had worked before when I wanted the ghost in the farmhouse to disappear, I was sure it would put an end to the horror of this demonic vision in the garden. However, the result was quite different this time. "Who are you to make such a commandment of me?" was the response from the shadow, equally precise and firm in its delivery.

The unspoken conversation between the entity and me that evening was brief and spirited. I shot back my wordless accusation that it was ugly, dark, and evil. Its reply charged me with poorly informed judgments and finished with a condemnation of humanity for the ignorant destruction done to the planet during our residence here. I received a barrage of non-verbal images of devastation and dark skies filled with overwhelming pollution. I saw leveled forests and colonies of starving people scraping the ground clear of all vegetation. I could hardly breathe as I stood there, receiving this communication in astonishment.

The being calmed now as if to allow me to regain my composure. As the stream of images faded, I began to breathe again and slowly realized the significance of this encounter. The lesson here was to halt judgment and keep my learned prejudices at bay while I experienced what was there to be seen and what was being communicated. For a moment, I felt strong in my ownership of choice in the experience. I was in control, acting from my own will. The power of this vision humbled me as a sense of tranquility returned.

In this trusting and accepting state of mind, I accepted the suggestion that it would show itself to me. I watched as the being began to slowly move from the shadow, sliding into a squat position beside the bush. It was confirmed; the ugliness of the grotesque face was even clearer to me now that the hunched figure stepped into the moonlight. My mounting dread was tempered only by the being's eyes, soft and sensitive to my reactions. I waited, unable to divert my gaze for even an instant.

"It's not my face," came the utterance from the entity, sitting quite still now in full view. With a barely discernable movement, the being exposed the terrifying mask as an inanimate cover, removable and intentional in its presence. When the being began to move the mask aside, I was taken by an exploding fear of what I was about to see. Cries to stop came rushing from my mind as terror overtook my entire being once again.

The movement stopped, and the mask slid back into place. I was gasping with horror, frozen to the spot, barely aware of the being's final counsel regarding my unreadiness. The encounter finished with a promise that it would return if I could set aside my judgment and condemnation of its kind. I was left with a feeling that the being wished to protect and guide me, even as I reflected a mass of unrelenting fear.

The power and energy faded from the shadow in the garden, and I fell onto the sofa next to me, weak from the feeling of extreme terror and shock. What had just happened? What was I so afraid to see? I realized then that my greatest fear—the fear I could not go beyond—was that the mask removed would reveal my *face looking back at me from the shadow. Or, worse still, that the being's actual face would be the same as the horrific mask.*

For more than a decade, my judgments would become the focus of a new exploration. I examined my fear of darkness, blackness, the others. I reflected on my reaction to ugliness without proof of evil, harm, hardness, or wrongdoing. I explored the fear of seeing myself in a frightful vision and inadvertently found a deeper knowledge of my soul nestled in a greater universal perspective. I had witnessed a spiritual ally, and the experience had meaning, mystery, and power.

Much later, I found references to these beings in the lore of some tribal and ancient cultures, from Bali to Tibet to the American native traditions. The commanding, wrathful nature of this ally, accompanied by its benevolent message, leads to the certain realization that to encounter such a being is, indeed, a moment of particularly good fortune—a blessing.

I think it was not a demon at all.

Humans might turn to outside conditions, personified natural forces, invisible gods, or misunderstood persons and groups as the cause of suffering, lighting a path to hell. Images and metaphors suggest it is necessary to resist the darkness to be in the light. There is a bias embedded, fortified by fear. Evil, or the perception of this quality during a supernatural experience, may be a projection stemming from beliefs.

When I define evil as an outside spiritual force, I find it difficult to make sense of the rules. Encountering something utterly unexpected and unlike myself initiates a fear for my soul. Evaluating with prejudice against certain characteristics affects my ability to see clearly. Challenging the forbidden, I use logic to move past this fear of the imagined look of evil. Darkness doesn't seem to naturally indicate evil.

These mostly unguided times challenged my opinion concerning evil and what I had been taught to believe. While some people's ignorance and diabolical wickedness will remain as dreadful as ever, the frightful realms of the supernatural are more accessible when viewed against a backdrop of strength in life and an all-encompassing oneness.

Encountering supernatural beings is an adventure full of unexpected choices, each one affecting the outcome. I sometimes stumble upon an unavoidable fright while walking alone at night. Each time I do, my notions regarding evil are put to the test.

Evil on the Adjacent Hill

I don't remember the exact purpose of my walk on the sparsely forested slopes of the California hills. I walked in the moonlight with a companion whose name I have forgotten. As was my habit, I eventually separated from this company so that I might listen. "Just up there, in the clearing."

From this knoll I could see the rolling buttocks of lower hills, shy of trees while lush with vegetation. I listened and watched the moon silently float above the wispy clouds in the sky. Slowly scanning the area with a soft focus and listening to the patterns of the sounds, I opened myself to the subtle influences of nature and the moment.

That is the way I often begin a walk, by noticing the textures. Sound, light, shapes, and shadows mingle with breezes and the movement of clouds. On a nearby knoll of similar proportions, I was finally able to feel a presence. Excitedly, I immediately decided to get closer to see more clearly. I was certain something was up there.

I charged off in the direction of the dense shadows atop the adjacent hill. Then, my breath suddenly jolted back into my lungs. I was stopped in my tracks. My heart still beats rapidly as I remember the instant of terror that night. I had seen nothing horrific, yet my body seized as if I had confronted a force greater than any encountered so far.

Stuck to that spot on the knoll, I freed my breath to regain motion and surveyed the hilltop next to me. It seemed darker, with more trees near the top. Moonlight created shadows clumping around the boulders of the rock outcrop near the peak. I chose not to allow the darkness of the shadows beneath the trees to affect me as I listened in the direction of the most powerful feelings of dread, watching the shadows with as much clarity and fearlessness as I could muster.

I could make out movement and change in the shadow. The dimensions seemed to fluctuate, shifting in size and contour. It seemed to expand when I felt its attention turning toward me, huffing and puffing with a sense of radical hysteria at having been seen. This posturing was enough to startle me into that familiar frozen terror, blood rushing from my cheeks and heart pounding with anticipation.

I consciously released my breath and continued watching without approaching or turning back. The contrast of the sky against the gradients of darkness exposed an uncanny sight. Here, this seemingly angry or irritable concentration of intelligence, or perhaps personality—paced back and forth, sometimes taller than the trees and at other times just blowing them aside as it moved beneath the branches.

I was witnessing a spirit entity behaving in such a way as to scare me nearly out of my wits — perhaps it was something evil. Regaining my composure, I ventured a more sensible approach to spirit watching and realized that frightening me away was the intention, not necessarily the underlying essence of the being itself.

Neither benevolent nor particularly malevolent, this entity simply did not want to interact with me. I had been determined to investigate before the fearful display summarily dismantled my plan. This was an intentional and successful ploy, and it was entirely congruent with what I had concluded about evil so far.

I now think of this type of spirit as an angry old man whose door I just broke down in my trouncing about. He's ranting and raving, and I'm standing there wondering why he's so angry, door crumpled on the floor, TV babbling in the background. I may even think he's evil, aggressively waving about with loud, threatening language. Yes, I could make a story *about the evil old man. Or I could choose to witness the situation from a different point of view, bearing my responsibility, learning respect for the presence of the other.*

I avoided the knoll and its powerful resident that night. Later, unsettled by the unresolved experience, I wondered if it had been a gathering of spirit energy or one entity guarding a secret, celebrating an event, or protecting a sacred place. I considered the possibility that it was the spirit of one deceased person, shape-shifting in the moonlight, undisturbed by my terrified presence.

I left this place and have no recollection of where in California I would look to find that hilltop today. I would have liked to try to witness its secret again at another time.

I think it may have been a sense of privacy and indignation that caused the huffing and the puffing of this supernatural entity. I had the option to decide if I wanted to keep going for the sake of learning about this powerful personality or to go elsewhere.

It seems likely that so-called evil spirits, when left undisturbed, hang around an earthly crossover position resisting passing information, fortune, blessings, health, or wellbeing to humans. Although neutral, they can have unpleasant defenses against being disturbed.

I don't imagine all supernatural entities are here to serve or interact with me. When I sense that I am too frightened of a threatening energy, there is usually no reason to go into its field.

Doing so suggests an unawareness, disrespect, and unwillingness to compromise my own path to allow for another's.

What I see and what I feel may be triggered by what I think. I watch and listen, knowing even a terrifying vision could be an ally making a point, getting my attention, or using an analogy to teach. I am not afraid to question my ideas about evil.

"I do not concern myself with gods and spirits, either good or evil, nor do I serve any."

- Lao Tzu

CHAPTER 5
Protection from What Frightens

When the feeling of dread is strong and starts to overcome my senses, I am aware I have abandoned the doctrines. Now I have to choose an authentic response, controlling fear as it surfaces, giving myself time to evaluate the source. In whatever manner I might become frightened, I, at least, intend to protect myself from being frightened by the mere look of it.

I thought I had handled most of my fear regarding strange and powerful visions. I rarely experienced overwhelming terror and took every opportunity to uncover a new encounter when and where I thought I might find one. The accidental encounter in this next story put my belief regarding evil spirits through yet another round of scrutiny.

Ghost in Southern France

In 1977, my husband and I were living and working in Algeria, North Africa. During a break at the university where my husband was teaching, we traveled with our five-month-old son and a couple of friends across the Mediterranean to southern France to kick off a summer excursion in Europe.

Veronique had insisted we visit the picturesque French village where she and her husband had purchased a historic home before joining the foreign cooperative efforts in Algeria. This destination was an hour or so north of Marseille and then east for some distance to a small village. I have no recollection of the name of the hamlet. It was late in the day when we landed at the airport, had a bite of dinner, and started on our drive through the countryside.

When we arrived at the village, I first noticed the enchanting stone walls towering particularly close to the road. Lining both sides, surrounded by weeds and climbing bushes, the ancient walls crumbled in some places and stood erect in others. The car's headlights created the illusion of a long tunnel enveloped in shadowy darkness as we drove slowly along the narrow road.

It appeared that the dwellings were sparsely inhabited, as evidenced by a few dimly lit windows beyond the stone walls. Jacque drove us further into the center of the village along what was now an even narrower dirt road, intermittently bordered by fences and broken gates suggesting previously owned private homes. Winding its way through leaning structures, overgrown and barely discernable in the night, the road wound in a loose coil until it finally opened to a broad parking place in front of an abandoned house.

We eyed the moss-stained dwelling. Its crumbling plaster revealed time-worn masonry. Narrow and tall, fronted with an unkempt garden and chipped iron fence, it stood among dry weeds, towering above the barren packed earth of the former grounds.

In the shadowy darkness falling on us now, we could make out what seemed to be an attached decaying structure around to the right and toward the back of the building. The fallen stones from the walls of that adjoining structure lay in heaps among the shambles of rotted beams and scraggly bushes. A withering tree completed the dreadfully dreary sight of Jacque and Veronique's home.

Inside, the atmosphere was chilly and damp. The floors and walls were all stone with pieces of plaster heaped along the room's edges, long since having fallen from the walls. Dust filtered into the cobwebs, noticeably settling on the few items of furniture left behind. Nothing about the items in the room suggested they might be sturdy enough or comfortable enough to sit in.

We marveled at the ancient home. Old pictures hung in uneven alignment and a single bare bulb dangled from a high ceiling casting a minimal amount of light over the room. A large wooden hatch in the floor just to the left of the center of the room added an unusual mystique to the place and prompted our notice and curiosity. We learned it covered a well that had been drained several times, even though it kept filling again with water not good to drink. Veronique seemed uninterested in talking about the well, even as the hatch's heavy, rotting wood and rusty iron hardware seemed impossible to ignore.

In the back of the main room, a secondary wall extended halfway across and ended abruptly. Only as we moved further into the room, clearing the entryway, were the narrow stairs it protected revealed. Briefly, we talked about the nearly empty room as Jacque casually escorted us to the stairwell. As I stood closer to the primitive hatch in the floor, I could feel a drafty chill on my ankles, contributing to a palpable experience of an ancient French dwelling.

Jacques and Veronique headed up the steep stairs. As I followed, I quickly straightened the crooked pictures hanging in an uneven arrangement on the wall, lending a bit of order to the neglected scene. The configuration of the staircase turned sharply at ninety-degree angles twice, effectively blocking the light from that single bulb downstairs as we climbed the steep, narrow steps to the second floor.

The stairwell offered no banisters or windows, so I felt a bit claustrophobic in the dimness of the light and the closeness of the high walls on both sides. There was no view of the room below or the room above as we continued single file up the stairs.

As we reached the top, whispering nervously about the single flashlight, my eyes adjusted just enough to see a large room with an oddly angled ceiling and long narrow windows. Our host located an unremarkable table lamp and switched it on, dispelling some of my apprehension.

The small bulb illuminated a room furnished in dusty antique furniture flavored sparsely with mid-twentieth century accents. The whole room seemed dingy and cheerless, with too many obscure corners and musty shadows. In short, it was a creepy house on an evening growing darker with the passage of time.

Quite matter-of-factly, Veronique announced that she and Jacque would be staying with friends in a nearby residence while my husband, the baby, and I would be settled in for the night in the empty house.

Smiling warmly, she turned to look directly at me as she assured us there was plenty of bedding and we would be quite comfortable until their return early the following day. There was, after all, only one bed in the house.

Adventures are often spontaneous and unexpected, so the discomfort I felt at the idea of staying in the old house without our hosts was quickly disregarded in favor of maintaining flexibility in the moment. I smiled with a courteous acceptance of our good fortune. Indeed, I would never forget the accommodation in this authentic French country house.

Veronique pounded and dusted a mattress with some help from the men. Then she spread several clean blankets over freshly smoothed sheets taken from a trunk at the foot of the bed. The linen had been thoughtfully placed in plastic when the couple had closed the house before leaving for Algeria, suggesting that every effort had been made to provide an inviting stay. It looked as though we would be warm and comfortable for the night.

Jacque assured us he would return in the morning to pick us up, and we would all head back to Marseille to begin the vacations we had planned. We had no water except the bottle we brought and no light except the single table lamp near the stairs. There was a toilet in a closet-sized room, although I dared not contemplate its general cleanliness and working order. We were young and adventurous and felt fortunate to find ourselves in this unique setting so completely unspoiled by tourism.

Once we were alone, my husband expressed his surprise at our friends' unexpected exit. In their haste, they had neglected the pleasantry of showing us around. The full extent of the house was still a mystery as the room fell into shadowy darkness, reflecting the final glow of the evening sky through the smudged square window panes. We shared an excited eagerness to explore the old building in the morning light as we settled the baby between us and slid into the clean bedding. The long day finally eclipsed the marginal concerns we shared as we drifted into sleep.

Sometime during the night, I was awakened by the sounds of the house—banging and scraping, thumping downstairs in the stairwell and somewhere behind the antique chest near the head of the bed. As I lay frozen with fearful apprehension, barely willing to take a breath, I realized my husband and son were, surprisingly, sleeping through it. They were unaffected by the noises, and I was thankful for that. I lay quietly frozen with fear, listening, quivering, barely breathing as the sounds continued, sometimes simultaneously from different areas of the empty house.

Finally, I remembered to practice what I had learned in previous encounters. I let go of my breath, concentrating on a complete rhythmic exhale, letting the air back in on its own accord, forcing the exhale again. As I began to breathe more regularly, I could feel control returning to my limbs and thoughts.

I began to listen carefully for the exact sounds, imagining reasonable explanations and noticing everything I could about the location and conditions. It seemed the pictures on the wall downstairs were banging and scraping. During this heightened state *of awareness, I first noticed the silent figure near the window at the far end of the bedroom.*

The specter was long and flowing in full manifestation. Within the wispy veil of the presence, I could see a shadowy face and a long ethereal illumination. This was the most solidly visible apparition I had ever seen. I was terrified, unable to move, and barely breathing. As I watched the flowing edges of the image, the inherently faint misty glow obscured the details of an appendage slowly reaching out towards me.

I couldn't determine more than that as I was now quite alarmed. I sat up, concentrating on breathing past my growing terror of having been seen by this personality. Unable to look away, I struggled to perceive what was there without filling in details with the imagined ideas flooding my mind, enhancing my terror.

The practice of the art of seeing, at that moment, was to breathe, be perceptive and quiet imagination. I resisted giving the vision a name or adding details of something thought rather than perceived. I still remember the dread I felt as I locked my gaze on the changing expressions of the apparition.

In my other encounters, the face of the specter had not been discernable. This time, it was the apex of my experience. I didn't have to ask myself if I was sure this vision was a separate autonomous entity rather than a projection from within my own self. There was nothing familiar about these features and personality. I hardly had time to consider it. The specter was coming closer.

"What are you doing here? Get out!" was the meaning and tone of the silent message emanating from the seemingly malevolent entity. My terror, having briefly been calmed by the breathing and controlled memories, was radically rekindled. I was once again frozen, unable to move, unable to breathe.

To my surprise, an intensity suddenly rose from the seat of my being. "We are here now. You get out!" burst my silent reply as I put all my mental strength into the command, pulling the power of life into the room, feeling as impenetrable and as forceful as I have ever felt. I followed my unconditional demand with the assurance that we would leave the next day, and the building would be as it was. The floating, changing specter began to fade.

As I trembled under the covers and regained my mobility, I woke my husband and asked if he was all right. The baby was still asleep. I told him I'd seen a ghost, and he bolted up to see. It was gone, of course. The noises had stopped, and the room was still and chilly. We talked about the spooky house as he easily drifted back to sleep, seemingly undisturbed by what I had seen. Eventually, I returned to a restless sleep myself, awake more often than not throughout the night.

Early the following day, Jacque and Veronique returned to pick us up. I thought I might have a better look around during the daytime, but our companions' sense of urgency abruptly vanquished this idea. There was no time for investigation or even to contemplate the uneven alignment of the pictures I had straightened the day before. The idea of discussing the event reminded me of the uncomfortable silliness often generated by sharing such things with others, so I kept quiet about it. We were quickly ushered out the door and on our way.

On the journey back to Marseille, Veronique asked how our night had been. My husband looked at me as if to suggest I go ahead and tell her what had happened. She picked up the nuance of the glance and turned in her seat. "What exactly happened?" she asked. I could tell by her heightened interest that she knew full well what had happened.

As I relayed the story, our friends interjected their stories of experiences in the house. The haunting of the dwelling was the reason it was purchased for very little money. It was also why the couple could not live there or stay there even for one night. With all their savings tied up in this haunted house that no one would buy, they had chosen to go to Algeria, where we met.

The story reported to me that morning was a sadistic schoolmarm, hung by the townspeople for her abuse and even murder of young children. The attached school had been destroyed two hundred years earlier, and the house itself was mostly uninhabitable. The stories went on to tell of the bell in the abandoned church that tolls on certain nights and of witches and mysterious happenings on the surrounding hillsides. There is apparently a great deal of lore attached to this little village.

My husband, my son, and I went on toward Nice for our vacation. Jacque and Veronique went off to visit their friends and family in the north. There wasn't any more to it than that—simply a lasting impression

I will never forget. We declined the offer to purchase the home at a steeply discounted price.

Restate your purpose in the face of what you fear. Stand your ground when questioned. If denied audience, reevaluate.

Encountering the ghost in southern France strengthened my sense of protection. I came to understand the necessity of feeling confident in the power of my own life. I am the greater force as I am embodied. When I know this, there is nothing I have to do to be protected.

My conviction kept the terror from overtaking me that night at that moment. I truly believed that my spirit in life was more powerful than any disembodied entity. This was an exponential jump in awareness. I finally realized the difference between needing to do something to protect myself from an evil spirit and simply being impenetrable by virtue of life and intention.

During the next few years, I discovered I could share what I was seeing with other people. This prompted me to begin a practice as a vision quest guide in the early eighties. As a guide, I was responsible for the safety of small groups of people as I led them into wilderness areas in search of encounters with the supernatural.

The gripping terror on the night of this next story threatened to derail the entire quest for our small band of seekers. Breathing was of no help as we stood unable to move, faced with a new challenge of strength and foreboding.

The Specter at the Bridge

At the time of this encounter, I was in full swing as a vision quest guide, spreading the word that I was willing to do walks into the woods to see something magical. I offered a money-back guarantee and required an informative seminar just before any walk.

I posted a little notice during a conference at Desert Hot Springs, and four people signed up for the evening walk into Joshua Tree National Monument. The casual engagement began when we drove out to the desert that very evening. Since the psychedelic experience was not a part of the vision quests I led, no formal behaviors and planning were necessary.

I'd never been to Joshua Tree, so I had no idea what to expect. In fact, as was common for me at the beginning of these walks, I didn't know what we would see or if we'd see anything at all. "If you don't see anything, all you have to do is ask for a refund at the end of the night," I clearly stated during the initial conversations.

The notion that we had discussed the possibility of nothing happening from the very beginning lessened my stress. After all, the spirit entities we were seeking are not at my command. I was happy to refund if any of the participants left feeling less than awed and surprised.

A young man, his wife, and a mother with her adolescent son made up the group. We started with some talk about the practice of the art of seeing. There was a meditation on the desert, the wind, and the sky. We each silently stated our purpose, an important part of the quest, and the mood was set.

We waited for the illuminated pathways to appear, listening for an invitation. I had no idea where the magic would be found that night in that place in the desert. The numerous rock formations and the eerie sense of stark quietness rising from the desert seemed inviting in any direction.

Following illuminated pathways is an essential step in this process for finding a supernatural presence. Standing quietly, I found an entry position and scanned the area for a visible response to my unspoken request. I envisioned being guided by whatever intelligence might hear and understand me.

It often starts as filtered moonlight reflecting off the lightly colored dust of a more heavily traveled path in the landscape. At the beginning of a walk, my mental tabulator is at work, explaining every subtle quality of the experience.

Spirit watching is practiced, in part, by letting go of this mental concern for the cause of the illumination. In my practice, I allow myself time to rationalize. Then, I follow the magic of the moment. We followed. We watched, using periphery vision as we listened intently to the silence between the sounds of nature.

The illuminated path we chose that night meandered along a crest and dropped to a dry stream bed. The ditch etched its way between the hills and across the flat to a wooden bridge. The darkness of the shadowy depth beneath the bridge lent its own creepiness to the scene.

There was a flat extension of outcrop jutting from the bank to the left of the gully, moderately high on a small cliff. A large flat stone protruded conspicuously from the crumbling hillside, creating a shadowed opening beneath it. Standing beside the hollow was a tall, dark specter, stern and still.

I was out front, ahead of the rest of the group by several yards when I first noticed it. The image startled me, and a squeak of a scream escaped. Stopping myself from an audible expression, I watched the figure as I continued into the ravine, skin prickling over my skull and down my arms. I remember breathing consciously to control my terror as I slowly walked toward the bridge.

The communication was meant to frighten. This spectral form did not want me to come near; that much was clear. A foreboding essence saturated my senses with dread. I stopped, frozen to the spot. My lungs were willing to let the air in and out, although my legs would not answer my commands to keep moving.

I imagined I saw the wispy flow and humanlike features of a tall native, protecting a grave from discovery. The entity's power was great, and the intention was clear -— protection through fear. Much went through my mind in that frozen moment, although I cannot declare that all of what I thought to be was actually there. I can only report that I saw the source of a *powerfully repelling energy center, existing in an apparently stationary form above our path.*

I wanted to run from the horrific image I imagined on the hillside that night. I was the leader, and we had to walk over that bridge if we were to be guided by the invitation bringing us this way in the first place. Clear pathways had been laid before us, and I knew to trust the illumination. I simply had to persist in my effort to move forward, across the bridge, regardless of this one repulsive force.

The near paralytic terror continued as I forced an approach to the wooden planks of the short bridge. "Just keep breathing," I thought. "Stay calm, autonomous."

I concentrated on exhaling fully and allowing the air to enter my lungs on its own, forcing my chest to expand and contract. I was breathing. Still, my limbs were slow to respond. I stopped and waited with the silent dignity required of a leader on a quest.

Shortly, one of the women in the group caught up with me. She obviously felt something too, as she declined my polite invitation to go ahead in front to the bridge. Although I did not mention the specter at this point, it was clear she, too, had felt the piercing warning as well. Spontaneously, I reached for her hand to lead her across the bridge with unified fortification. It didn't work. Neither of us was able to go any further, separately or together.

Next to arrive by our side was her son. She didn't hesitate to reach for his hand as we again began to step forward. Something had changed. The moment his energy was added to ours, a sense of diffusion eased the powerlessness, making it easy to cross the bridge and continue our journey. When we were past the area of intensity, I turned to see the last two members of our group. The couple held hands and easily walked across the planks with only the reasonable hesitancy one might expect upon facing a poorly aged bridge.

The relative strength of this entity seemed to present an opportunity for learning something about what others were witnessing, if anything. Everyone reported a noticeable sensation of discomfort while crossing the bridge that night. I shared my experience.

When I suggested a spectral presence, they could see it, and there was a bustle of astonishment and excitement. My promise of a supernatural encounter had been delivered. My interest in objectivity, however, had been a bit thwarted. As a practitioner, I savored the moment when there was a recognition of an undeniable force without suggestion or prompting.

We quickly turned our attention back to the illumination, continuing our quest through the rocky moonlit landscape. This specter was not the apex of our journey in the desert that night. The illuminated path extended beyond the bridge and over the next hill.

There seemed to be alchemy between male and female that strengthened the courage of the entire party. Perhaps a synergized vibration signaled the nonchallenging status of our group. A distinct change had occurred. It allowed the grip of fear to dissipate, making it possible to pass.

Sometimes I feel I haven't enough courage. When my imagination mingles with perception, frightening visions can accompany my heightened sensitivity. By controlling creative enhancements during encounters, some of the judgments challenging my clarity as witness are dispersed.

Chants on the Trail

Walking alone in the night through a forested area can sometimes be creepy. A rustle of leaves may spawn images of wild predators, and a heightened sense of alertness can stimulate remembered images of fictional threats. My intention is always to walk quietly, listening, breathing, noticing everything, attaching to nothing, looking for spirit beings, and allowing them to be near.

There was a time when I became obsessed with the notion that I was being followed. On some evenings during this frightening period, I heard footsteps behind me while walking along a familiar path I had traveled dozens of times before without incident.

The first time I heard the footsteps, I stopped and turned around, expecting a friendly encounter with another member of the small community where I lived. There was no one there. Of course, I thought the sounds of footsteps must have been my imagination. As I continued along my way, I heard the heavy footsteps behind me again. I looked, and again there was no one there.

I hastened along the path until I noticed the sounds of heavy footsteps had ceased. It was a frazzling incident that could have been quickly forgotten had it ended there.

The next night, I decided to walk through the woods again, practicing seeing whatever was there to be seen. The first part of the walk seemed normal enough. I was relaxed and going about my process of listening intently as I slowly moved along the dark trail. That's when I heard the sounds again, like the night before, a few yards behind me.

This time I was more inwardly alarmed as I continued walking. My heartbeat increased, goosebumps riffling up my arms, and my breath required conscious control. I wondered what threat was stimulating these physical reactions. I couldn't see anything when I turned around. If I stopped, the thudding stopped. If I sped up, so did the sounds behind me. Again, I practically ran out of the forest.

A few days later, I decided to attempt another night walk. Having been so terrified on the previous adventure, I thought this might be a situation requiring I "get back on the horse as soon as possible."

Against all my efforts to control fear, I had been frightened out of the woods twice. This didn't make sense and was perhaps associated with an imaginary idea. There was a mystery to discover in this uncomfortable experience.

This time, I decided to carefully describe what I heard and felt, restricting my thoughts about what it sounded like and avoiding extrapolating what it must be. Initially, I let my mental regimen look for ways to explain the sounds in tangible terms. I checked my daypack for loose straps or dangling flaps. I looked for ways my walk, clothing, or manner were different when the sounds were behind me and when they weren't. Soon the characteristics of the experience became more distinguishable.

There was an unseen boundary past which the sounds could not be heard. Within the confines of those imaginary boundaries, the thudding sounds behind me seemed to be about ten feet back, sometimes closing in to just a few terrifying feet from my back.

Turning around and seeing nothing only enhanced my discomfort. So, I stopped trying to see. Instead, I concentrated on slow, steady breathing and attentive listening. The thudding sounds persisted, louder than the pounding of my heart, more audible than my own boots on the trail. Relief would come, I knew, when I crossed the defined boundaries of the phenomenon.

My curiosity pushed me to continue while my expectation of terror insisted I did not. Confused and full of nearly uncontrollable fear, I had the idea that if I could not calm myself, my night walks and spirit watching explorations were over.

I had evidence that evil spirits can't hurt me and likely don't exist. During this terrifying time, I thought of the Oneness I turn to when nothing else seems to be working. I thought of the power of the life force and remembered the kindness in the eyes of the ally rising from the shadow in the garden. I felt my stability above the molten core of the planet beneath my feet.

A mantra came to me.
> *There's a light that shines above me.*
> *There's a light that shines below.*
> *There's a light that surrounds me*
> *Everywhere I go.*

I began to chant these lines in the face of this unknown force. I thought I had accidentally attracted a fearsome entity or had released an inner demon to contend with.

I was immediately released from the vulnerable place of reactive fright. I felt strong and protected on all levels. Nothing supernatural from above or below could manifest to shake my certainty that I held my life force as a shield of light around me.

This challenging experience went on for a few weeks until a chance meeting with a trance medium resulted in information I could use. A clingy gargoyle of some sort had apparently spotted me. I was told it was of no particular significance, simply a bother and a distraction. The channeled spirit spoke through a willing host and assured me he would get rid of it for me.

I didn't experience the sounds of footsteps along the trail again. I don't know what they were since I didn't see anything during this odd run of events. What I gained was the mantra. I use it now as a song to utter when I feel the unidentified presence of that which frightens.

Unlike a talisman, I knew a chant would never be left behind or be taken from me. It was faster than meditation and could range from a mere comforting thought to a loud defending chorus. The greater concepts inherent in the verse melt doubt and aloneness above the heavens, below the ground, and all around me, with each breath I take. This chant proved to be a valuable tool in my explorations.

Since this part of the *Spirit Watching* series is focused on conquering fear, these stories have naturally been the ones that frightened me most. To my surprise, the terrifying encounters dwindled as I became more aware of my place in nature. Courage came when I needed it.

Over the years, I began to question these supernatural experiences. I thought visions of other-dimensional beings could be a projection of my inner self. Perhaps the visions were tapping into deeply held archetypical images seated in the collective human subconscious.

Naturally, understanding perception and imagination became the next focus in my quest to witness the presence of spirit beings. I had conquered most of my fear. Next, I would hone an ability to see more clearly. I began to develop techniques to quiet the chatter of my mind, subduing dogma, memory and imagination. Not deciding what I was seeing expanded possibilities and vastly increased the occurrence of supernatural encounters.

AFTERWORD

For millions of young people venturing beyond the lines of mainstream religion, fiction is beginning to define spirituality and the supernatural almost entirely. Perception of deep nature seems to have a slower, more subtle frequency than what is necessary when interfacing with electronic images. The ability to see spirit entities may be slated for the evolutionary slush pile, unless we quiet ourselves enough to witness what's there to be seen.

For now, it seems there are spirit beings. This is not a snipe hunt or Santa story. *Spirit Watching* invites you to relax and see; seek them yourself if you like. You might choose to keep them away or invite them in, ignore them, or simply accept that supernatural entities are near you. The central point of my practice is the willingness to allow what is there to be seen without attaching imagination, dogma, and myth.

Of course, as a skeptic, I consider all of the possibilities. If my postulate concerning the existence of spirit beings is wrong, at least my mission to allow the encounters will have personal value. It will have allowed me the chance to examine images manifesting from deep within my subconscious. Either way, here is an opportunity to entertain an alternative perspective.

I propose that on the edge of our awareness, there is information traveling through other dimensions. If we want to, and we practice, we can become more mindful of entities existing on that edge and perhaps gain wisdom from the resulting interaction.

"There are things known and there are things unknown, and in between are the doors of perception."

Aldous Huxley

ABOUT THE AUTHOR

Catherine Espara is a skeptic who, since childhood, has had to account for thrilling and terrifying encounters with other-dimensional beings.

The quest to understand the supernatural engulfed an entire lifetime. Catherine became an explorer, developing her art as witness and participant, engaging a lifelong silent passion of allowing supernatural entities into her awareness with as much clarity as possible. She writes with honesty and freedom, considering thoughtful parameters, using only firsthand accounts.

Recently Catherine retired in California to assemble stacks of journals and stories into a chronicle of discoveries. Focusing on fear, perception and practice, Espara tells of the circumstances surrounding her intention to witness supernatural entities. There is an invitation in her writing, encouraging readers to see for themselves.

APPRECIATIONS

Laura, your gifts fortify mine in unexpected ways. Nikki, your unwavering support exceeded our coaching mandate a hundred times over, and still you share your expertise generously. And Terri, the ultimate encourager. I needed all of you.

I owe gratitude to my sons, Sebastian and Tyler, who weathered such a mother. And a general appreciation goes to my mom and all the friends who have been supportive for decades as I promised my book on the Art of Seeing; Visions of Magic; Not So Invisible; and finally entitled, *Spirit Watching, Part I.*

SPIRIT WATCHING
Learning to See Ghosts, Earth Spirits and Others

Part I — FIRST, CONQUER FEAR

In an effort to understand what was happening when I was seeing the ghost in the old farmhouse, I practiced freeing my breath and scanning the darkness with a soft, diffused focus. From this one purposeful act blossomed an array of frightening supernatural experiences. Thus, began my inquiry into fear, relying on myself as the subject and the observer.

Part II — NEXT, HONE PERCEPTION

Exploring the difference between perception and imagination became my next obsession. I began to develop techniques to quiet the chatter of my mind, subduing dogma, memory and imagination. Not deciding what I was seeing opened possibilities regarding the nature of spirit beings. My boundaries expanded, vastly increasing the occurrences of supernatural encounters.

Part III — THEN, PRACTICE

Wanting to see more, I noticed the location, timing, and purpose that would produce the most reliable results. Becoming sensitive to the sublime powers of the spinning globe, the sky, wind and stone, I naively explored supernatural phenomena with curiosity—allowing the unknown, trusting in a sense of Oneness. These are the techniques I found useful.

Printed in the United States
by Baker & Taylor Publisher Services